THE Sublime
RESTAURANT COOKBOOK

FLORIDA'S ULTIMATE DESTINATION FOR VEGAN CUISINE

Nanci Alexander

BOOK PUBLISHING COMPANY
Summertown, Tennessee

Library of Congress Cataloging-in-Publication Data

Alexander, Nanci.
    The Sublime Restaurant cookbook / Nanci Alexander.
        p.   cm.
    Includes index.
    ISBN 978-1-57067-227-9
1. Vegetarian cookery.   2. Sublime Restaurant.   I. Title.

    TX837.A3765 2009
        641.5'636—dc22

                                                2008040979

Cover and interior photos: *Warren Jefferson*
Cover and interior design: *Aerocraft Charter Art Service*

Printed in Canada

Book Publishing Company
P.O. Box 99
Summertown, TN 38483
888-260-8458
www.bookpubco.com

ISBN 978-1-57067-227-9

17 16 15 14 13 12 11 10 09   1 2 3 4 5 6 7 8 9

Book Publishing Co. is a member of Green Press Initiative.
We chose to print this title on paper with postconsumer
recycled content, processed without chlorine, which saved
the following natural resources:

46 trees

2,135 pounds of solid waste

16,624 gallons of wastewater

4,005 pounds of greenhouse gases

32 million BTU of total energy

For more information, visit www.greenpressinitiative.org.

Paper calculations from Environmental Defense Paper Calculator,
www.papercalculator.org

BOOK
PUBLISHING
COMPANY

green
press
INITIATIVE

Contents

This book is dedicated

to all the animals who

are thought of as food

instead of the magnificent

individual beings they are.

Their suffering has not

gone unnoticed; in fact,

it has shown us the depths

of our compassion and

awakened us to a way

of life in which we respect

all of Earth's creatures.

Acknowledgments

Thanks first and foremost to Shawn Raval for managing every detail of the entire project and turning the idea for this cookbook into tangible reality.

To Sublime's chef and staff: a hearty round of applause for your dedication and diligence. Bravo to Jeremy Shock for inspiring us with his grand plans and to Lori Kirby for being the rock that we could lean on.

Finally, our deepest gratitude to our thousands of guests and friends: this book would not have been written without your support over the past five years.

Foreword

This book brings you the flavors and beauty of Sublime, one of the world's truly great restaurants. As soon as you walk in the door, you'll know Sublime is a special place with its waterfalls, greenery, Peter Max paintings, and smart, attentive staff. As you walk to your table, you may spot Hollywood celebrities, politicians, or famous musicians and artists.

Almost as soon as the restaurant opened its doors, it won the highest accolades from national and local press. Now you can bring it all home. This collection embodies the elegance of the restaurant itself.

Whether you are drawn to Mediterranean, Asian, or Latin influences, or more typical American fare, you will find it here. Each recipe is delightfully conceived and beautifully presented, yet surprisingly quick to prepare. The delicious Picatta, Orecchiette, Pad Thai, and down-home Mac and "Cheese" are ready in minutes.

But we're getting ahead of ourselves. Intrigue your taste buds with Mediterranean Polenta Squares, Stuffed Mushrooms, Potato Pancakes, Baba Ganoush, or Nori-Crusted Tofu. Continue the seduction with Frito Misto, Mushroom Ceviche, delicate Rice Paper Spring Rolls, or Fried Green Tomatoes.

Follow these with Carrot Ginger Soup, or perhaps Chilled Cucumber Coconut Soup, or White Bean and Escarole Soup—all are delicious. Next, a perfectly balanced salad, whether you choose Baby Arugula Salad, Watercress Salad, Tomato Carpaccio, or Caesar. Or make a simple Chopped Salad come alive with shallots, kalamata olives, a touch of garlic, and a splash of red wine vinegar.

I've already hinted at some of the main attractions. You might choose the Portobello Tenderloin or Grilled Seitan Steak, both of which put meat and potatoes to shame. But how about a new twist on pizza? Try Pizza Margherita, Forest Mushroom

Pizza, Florentine Pizza, or Seven-Layer Pizza. The Sublime pesto sauce (used on their Pesto Pizza) gives pizza sauce a whole new meaning.

But more than anything else, Sublime is known for the way it finishes off a meal with the most delectable desserts imaginable: S'mores Brownies, Coconut Cake, Georgia Peach Crisp, Baked Apple Napoleon, and Brown Rice Pudding.

There are two hidden ingredients that make every Sublime recipe truly special. The first is vibrant health. Many gourmet cookbooks delight the taste buds, only to make your bathroom scale groan. With each bite you can imagine how hard it's going to be to get into your clothes in the morning. Your cardiologist won't even want to speak with you.

Sublime knows that eating well means feeling good, too. Each recipe is prepared from the freshest and very best plant-derived ingredients. So, instead of worrying about cholesterol and animal fat, let your senses adore the wonderful flavors and your body delight in how good it feels.

Millions of people are now looking for healthful recipes that go beyond meaty, cheesy fare. Many follow vegetarian or vegan diets full time, and many more are moving in that direction. Science has proved them right. Research studies have shown that people who set aside animal products and build their meals from vegetables, fruits, grains, and legumes reach a level of health they never expected. Not only does extra weight melt away, but heart disease also reverses and diabetes improves dramatically; people with arthritis, migraines, and digestive issues find these problems fading into memory. This is part of the reason that animal products find no place in Sublime recipes. Quite the contrary, these meals are remarkable for the incredible nutrition they bring to your plate.

You'll also learn simple ways to lighten up your life. Looking to sauté without the oil and grease? Try Sublime's savory vegetable stocks instead. Weighed down by fat and calories? Try the Cashew Cream or Tofu Ricotta. Looking to save time? Nearly every recipe freezes easily and reheats perfectly. Are family members wedded to less-than-healthful foods? They will adore vegetables prepared the Sublime way.

Would you like sauces and toppings with a lighter touch? You'll find them here with the Onion Gravy, Lemon-Caper Sauce, Plum Sauce, Pesto Sauce, Stir-Fry Sauce, Salsa, Tzatziki Sauce, and endless others, all quickly and easily made.

Now, many in the Sublime crowd are too young to worry about their health. What they appreciate is the second ingredient hidden in every dish: compassion.

People concerned about the environment have long known that choosing a plant-based diet is the kindest thing you can do for the earth. Today's factory farms spew pollutants into rivers and greenhouse gasses into the atmosphere. Simply raising cattle, chickens, pigs, and other animals for food means growing acre after acre of feed grains and using enormous amounts of water (and often pesticides, as well) to yield products that contain only a fraction of the protein and energy that went into the animals.

Choosing a plant-based diet is also the kindest thing you can do for animals. Americans now eat, believe it or not, more than one million animals per hour. Do the math: that's more than nine billion every year, according to the U.S. Department of Agriculture. On their way to your plate, they are poked, prodded, and packed under grotesquely cruel conditions that would not be allowed even in prisons. A plant-based diet lets you set all these problems aside.

While your eyes delight in the magnificent colors and your taste buds rejoice in exquisite flavors, your waistline will be trimmer, and your heart will be lighter, too. I hope you enjoy these exquisite recipes. Each one is truly sublime.

Neal D. Barnard, MD

Introduction

The story of Sublime begins with that of its owner, Nanci Alexander. By nature a compassionate person, Nanci founded the Animal Rights Foundation of Florida (ARFF) in 1989 to help abused animals. Although volunteering as president of ARFF kept Nanci very busy, her love for animals kept driving her to seek new ways to help them.

The Victorian writer Mary Anne Evans once wrote, "I would not creep along the coast, but steer out in mid-sea, by guidance of the stars." And so in 1999, Nanci steered out into the restaurant business (heretofore uncharted territory for her), guided only by her convictions. Because animal agriculture represents the world's greatest source of animal cruelty, the most significant step one can take to reduce this abuse is to move to a plant-based diet. Nanci wanted to create a restaurant that would show that plant-based food could indeed be sublime.

Nanci's first step was to find the perfect location. She scoured all of South Florida (her home for most of her life) and settled on a prime spot in the heart of Fort Lauderdale. Next, she worked on drawing up designs and reviewing blueprints for a structure that would do justice to the exquisite foods she planned to offer. As construction was under way, Nanci meticulously planned all of the details to create an unforgettable, one-of-a-kind destination for food lovers. Four years of hard work later, Nanci's vision became a breathtaking reality: Sublime was born.

Sublime's subsequent success surpassed even Nanci's high expectations, garnering worldwide media mentions and superlative reviews. Guests ranging from herbivores to omnivores and health-food nuts to gastronomes all checked out what Sublime had to offer. Half a decade later, Sublime is still going strong, with devotees flocking to the restaurant on a daily basis. And since the day it opened, all of Sublime's profits have been donated to animal welfare organizations.

Just goes to show how far you can go when the stars guide you.

Shawn Raval

Hors d'oeuvres

Sublime's private room has had its share of glittering parties
(you may have heard about Pam Anderson's fortieth birthday bash).
Add a touch of glamour to your next shindig with this stupendous
selection of hors d'oeuvres. They're the perfect start for either
a cocktail party or as a prelude to a sit-down dinner.

This traditional recipe offers an authentic taste of the Middle East. Serve it on toasted pita bread triangles.

Baba Ganoush

YIELD: 4 TO 6 SERVINGS

1 large eggplant
(about 1 pound)

1 tablespoon
extra-virgin olive oil

1 bunch (about 3 ounces)
flat-leaf parsley, chopped

1 cup finely diced
red onion

2 tablespoons
freshly squeezed
lemon juice

2 tablespoons
minced garlic

1 tablespoon tahini

1 teaspoon
freshly ground
black pepper

1 teaspoon
ground cumin

Salt

Preheat the oven to 400 degrees F. Place the eggplant on a baking sheet and rub it all over with the oil. Bake for 45 minutes, until it is soft and cooked through. Cool to room temperature.

Slice the eggplant in half lengthwise and scoop out all of the flesh, leaving only the skin behind. Chop the eggplant flesh and combine it with the parsley, onion, lemon juice, garlic, tahini, pepper, and cumin in a large bowl. Season with salt to taste.

Serve immediately or thoroughly chilled. Stored in an airtight container in the refrigerator, leftover Baba Ganoush will keep for up to 5 days.

This bite-sized snack is at once exotic
and refreshing.

Nori-Crusted Tofu

YIELD: 4 TO 6 SERVINGS

1 pound extra-firm tofu,
rinsed, drained, and
patted dry

2 sheets nori, toasted
and finely chopped
in a spice grinder or
food processor

1 teaspoon wasabi paste

1 English cucumber
(about 1 pound), sliced
into ⅛-inch-thick rounds

Cut the tofu into ½-inch cubes. Roll the cubes in the nori until they are evenly coated all over. Place a dab of the wasabi paste to taste on each cucumber round and top it with a cube of the tofu.

Capers and basil infuse zing
into mellow polenta.

Mediterranean Polenta Squares

See photo between pages 22 and 23.

YIELD: 4 TO 6 SERVINGS

2 cups water

2 cups polenta
(yellow corn grits)

1 bunch fresh basil
(about 3 ounces),
thinly sliced

1 jar (4 ounces) capers,
drained and chopped

2 tablespoons
nutritional yeast flakes

2 tablespoons
vegan margarine

1 teaspoon salt

Line a baking sheet with parchment paper. Bring the water to a boil in a medium saucepan and slowly whisk in the polenta. Whisk continually until the mixture thickens. Stir in the basil, capers, nutritional yeast, margarine, and salt, mixing until evenly incorporated.

Pour the mixture evenly onto the prepared baking sheet and refrigerate until firm to the touch.

Transfer to a cutting board and slice into 1-inch-thick strips, then slice the strips into 1-inch squares.

Preheat the oven to 350 degrees F. Just before serving, place the squares in a sheet pan and bake for 5 minutes, until warm and slightly crispy. Serve hot.

An Old World classic gets a new twist.

Potato Pancakes

YIELD: 4 TO 6 SERVINGS

2 large russet potatoes,
peeled and grated

1 bunch fresh chives
(about 3 ounces), thinly sliced

1 small red onion, finely diced

4 tablespoons
Cashew Cream (page 84)

1 cup soy cream cheese

Salt

Freshly ground black pepper

White truffle oil (optional)

5 tablespoons vegan margarine

P lace the potatoes, chives, onion, and Cashew Cream in a large bowl and stir until evenly combined.

Place the soy cream cheese in a small bowl and season with salt, pepper, and white truffle oil, if using, to taste. Mix well and set aside.

Using a 1-ounce scoop (2 tablespoons) or a large spoon, press the potato mixture to drain off any excess liquid and form the mixture into about 12 small cakes.

Heat the margarine in a large skillet. Add the potato cakes in batches and cook on each side for about 3 minutes, or until golden brown.

Drain the cakes on paper towels and sprinkle them with salt and pepper to taste. Top each cake with a dollop of the reserved soy cream cheese mixture just before serving.

These delectable mushrooms are perfect for elegant gatherings.

Stuffed Mushrooms

YIELD: 4 TO 6 SERVINGS

12 (1-inch) mushrooms with stems (about 1 pound), cleaned

2 tablespoons extra-virgin olive oil

Salt

Freshly ground black pepper

4 tablespoons vegan margarine

1 cup finely chopped white onion

3 garlic cloves, minced

1 cup white wine

1 cup panko or regular breadcrumbs

1 bunch fresh chives (about 3 ounces), sliced

Preheat the oven to 350 degrees F. Remove the mushroom stems from the caps and set aside the stems. Starting from the underside of the mushroom cap, carefully peel off the outer layer of skin. Rub the peeled caps with the olive oil and sprinkle lightly with salt and pepper.

Place the caps in an 8-inch square baking pan and bake for 10 to 15 minutes, until tender. Drain and reserve any liquid released by the mushrooms and set the caps aside.

Chop the mushroom stems. Heat the margarine in a large sauté pan over medium heat. Add the onion and garlic and cook and stir for 2 to 3 minutes, until lightly golden. Add the mushroom stems and cook and stir for 5 minutes. Add the white wine and cook and stir for 2 to 3 minutes longer, until the mixture is almost dry.

Transfer to a medium mixing bowl and add the breadcrumbs, reserved mushroom liquid, and chives. Season with salt and pepper to taste and mix until well combined. Stuff the breadcrumb mixture into the mushroom caps.

Preheat the oven to 350 degrees F. Shortly before serving, arrange the stuffed caps (stuffing side up) on a baking sheet and bake for 8 to 10 minutes, until the stuffing is golden brown.

Sublime's success surpassed even high expectations . . . garnering worldwide media mentions and superlative reviews. Guests ranging from herbivores to omnivores and health-food nuts to gastronomes all check out what Sublime has to offer.

Appetizers

Patrons begin their enchanting dining experience at Sublime with our taste-bud-awakening appetizers. It's not unusual to see groups ordering two, three, and sometimes four different appetizers and passing them around. With such a diverse selection, it's hard to choose! Enjoy these appetizers before dinner or paired with a salad for a superb lunch.

Crunchy cauliflower is the star of
this sweet-and-spicy tempura dish.

Frito Misto

See photo between pages 22 and 23.

YIELD: 4 TO 6 SERVINGS

SWEET CHILI SAUCE

⅓ cup water

4 teaspoons minced garlic

2 teaspoons crushed
red chili flakes

⅓ cup white wine vinegar

⅓ cup sugar

1 teaspoon paprika

CAULIFLOWER TEMPURA

2 heads cauliflower
(about 4 pounds total),
florets only

4 cups Tempura Batter
(page 89)

GARNISH

2 tablespoons
chopped scallions

1 teaspoon
white sesame seeds

To make the Sweet Chili Sauce, combine the water, garlic, and chili flakes in a small saucepan and bring to a boil. Add the vinegar, sugar, and paprika. Simmer over low heat for about 15 minutes, until the mixture thickens slightly and is the consistency of syrup.

To make the Tempura while the sauce is simmering, dip the cauliflower florets into the batter until they are evenly coated. Deep-fry them in vegetable oil at 350 degrees F, until brown and crispy. Drain on paper towels. Gently toss the hot cauliflower with the Sweet Chili Sauce in a large bowl.

Preheat the oven to 350 degrees F. Spread the sesame seeds on a baking sheet and heat in the oven for 2 to 3 minutes, just until golden brown. Garnish the Cauliflower Tempura with the scallions and sesame seeds.

The unique textures of rice paper and sprouts are accentuated by a piquant plum sauce in this delightful cold appetizer. Look for rice paper at Asian grocery stores and in the Asian section of natural food stores and supermarkets.

Rice Paper Spring Rolls

YIELD: 4 TO 6 SERVINGS

PLUM SAUCE

½ pound fresh plums, pitted

¼ cup sugar

¼ cup rice vinegar

¼ cup plum wine or
sweet fruit wine

¼ teaspoon grainy mustard

SPRING ROLLS

12 sheets rice paper

1 cup bean sprouts

¼ cup shredded napa cabbage

¼ cup shredded bok choy

2 tablespoons
matchstick-sliced carrot

2 tablespoons
thinly sliced red onion

2 tablespoons
thinly sliced red bell pepper

GARNISH

2 tablespoons
chopped scallions

To make the Plum Sauce, combine the plums, sugar, vinegar, wine, and mustard in a medium saucepan and simmer over medium heat for 25 to 30 minutes, or until thick. Transfer to a blender and process until smooth.

To make the Spring Rolls, soak the rice paper sheets in warm water, 1 sheet at a time, until soft. Stack the rice paper sheets on a wet towel, separating each sheet with additional wet towels, and set them aside. Combine the bean sprouts, cabbage, bok choy, carrot, onion, and bell pepper in a large bowl.

Lay 1 rice paper sheet on a flat surface and arrange 2 tablespoons of the vegetable mixture at the bottom. Roll the sheet halfway, tuck the ends under, and finish rolling. Slice the roll in half at a sharp angle. Repeat the process with the remaining rice paper sheets. Garnish the sliced rolls with the scallions and serve with the Plum Sauce.

This Southern classic, accompanied by a lively corn sauté, gets a bold finishing touch of horseradish sauce.

Fried Green Tomatoes

YIELD: 4 TO 6 SERVINGS

HORSERADISH SAUCE

1 cup white wine

¼ cup chopped shallots

¼ cup prepared horseradish

½ cup vegan margarine

4½ teaspoons freshly squeezed lemon juice

Salt

FRIED GREEN TOMATOES

2 cups Tempura Batter (page 89)

3 large green tomatoes (about 1 pound), cut into ⅛-inch-thick slices

1 cup yellow cornmeal

Salt

Freshly ground black pepper

To make the Horseradish Sauce, place the wine, shallots, and horseradish in a small saucepan over high heat. Cook and stir for about 15 minutes, until almost dry. Transfer to a blender and process on high speed for about 2 minutes, or until smooth. Blend in the cold margarine, 1 tablespoon at a time. Pour the mixture into a glass or plastic container and stir in the lemon juice. Season with salt to taste and set aside.

To make the Fried Green Tomatoes, spread the cornmeal on a plate. Place the Tempura Batter in a large mixing bowl. Soak the tomato slices in the batter for 1 minute, then dip them in the cornmeal to coat both sides evenly.

Deep-fry the tomatoes in vegetable oil at 350 degrees F, until the crust is golden brown. Remove the tomatoes from the oil and sprinkle with salt and pepper to taste. Drain on paper towels and set aside.

CORN SAUTÉ

4 tablespoons
vegan margarine, chilled

¾ cup fresh corn

2 tablespoons finely
diced red bell pepper

2 tablespoons finely
diced red onion

2 tablespoons thinly
sliced scallion

GARNISH

½ cup micro greens
or mesclun

To make the Corn Sauté, heat the margarine in a sauté pan until it starts to brown. Add the corn and cook until it starts to snap and pop. Add the bell pepper, onion, and scallion and stir to combine.

To serve, top the Corn Sauté with the Fried Green Tomatoes. Drizzle with the Horseradish Sauce and garnish with the micro greens.

This Old Country favorite marries succulent breaded eggplant with luscious tomato sauce.

Eggplant Rollatini

YIELD: 4 TO 6 SERVINGS

GARLIC BUTTER

½ cup vegan margarine

6 tablespoons minced garlic

Salt

EGGPLANT ROLLATINI

1 large eggplant (1 pound),
cut lengthwise into
10 to 12 very thin slices

½ cup canola oil

Salt

Freshly ground black pepper

1½ cups Tofu Ricotta
(page 85)

2 cups all-purpose flour

1 quart plain soymilk

2 cups panko or
regular breadcrumbs

1 cup Basic Tomato Sauce
(page 92)

To make the Garlic Butter, place the margarine and garlic in a small saucepan and bring to a gentle simmer. Cook and stir over low heat for about 10 minutes, until the garlic is tender. Season with salt to taste and set aside.

To make the Eggplant Rollatini, brush the eggplant slices with the oil and sprinkle with salt and pepper to taste. Grill the eggplant over high heat (using a grill, cast iron skillet, or griddle) until soft, about 2 minutes per side. Let cool to room temperature. Place 2 tablespoons of the Tofu Ricotta on one end of each eggplant slice and roll it up to enclose the filling.

Place the flour in a shallow pan. Place the soymilk in another shallow pan. Place the breadcrumbs in a third shallow pan. Dip each eggplant roll first in the flour, then in the soymilk, and finally in the breadcrumbs until all the rolls are evenly coated all over.

Deep-fry 3 to 4 rolls at a time in vegetable oil at 350 degrees F until they are golden brown. Remove from the oil, sprinkle with salt and pepper to taste, and drain on paper towels.

To serve, spoon 2 to 3 tablespoons of the tomato sauce in a 3-inch circle on individual plates. Place the hot eggplant rolls on top. Drizzle with 1 to 1½ tablespoons of the Garlic Butter.

HERB SALAD (optional)

6 tablespoons sliced chives, cut into 1-inch lengths

2 tablespoons edible flower petals

2 tablespoons flat-leaf parsley leaves

2 tablespoons tiny basil leaves

To make the optional Herb Salad, combine all of the ingredients in a small bowl. Garnish each serving of Eggplant Rollatini with the Herb Salad.

A zesty marinade enlivens
this raw vegetable appetizer.

Mushroom Ceviche

YIELD: 4 TO 6 SERVINGS

CITRUS MARINADE

¾ teaspoon peeled and chopped fresh ginger

¾ teaspoon minced garlic

¼ cup sake

¼ cup freshly squeezed orange juice

2 tablespoons freshly squeezed lemon juice

1 tablespoon freshly squeezed lime juice

Salt

To make the Citrus Marinade, place the ginger and garlic in a clean cloth and squeeze out all the juice into a bowl. Discard the ginger and garlic pulp. Add the sake, orange juice, lemon juice, and lime juice. Season with salt to taste.

MUSHROOM CEVICHE

2 cups oyster mushrooms, stems removed

½ pint cherry tomatoes, halved

1 cup seeded and sliced cucumber

¾ cup diced avocado

¾ cup diced mango

½ cup sliced red onion

2 tablespoons sliced green bell pepper

2 tablespoons sliced red bell pepper

2 tablespoons sliced yellow bell pepper

GARNISH

1 tablespoon white sesame seeds

To make the Mushroom Ceviche, place the mushroom caps in the bowl with the marinade and let marinate at room temperature for at least 1 hour. Remove the mushrooms from the marinade and transfer them to a large bowl. Add the tomatoes, cucumber, avocado, mango, onion, and all of the bell peppers. Add the marinade and toss until the vegetables are evenly coated.

Preheat the oven to 350 degrees F. Spread the sesame seeds on a baking sheet and heat in the oven for 2 to 3 minutes, just until golden brown. Garnish each serving of Mushroom Ceviche with the sesame seeds.

Soups

Sublime's soups are always prepared from the finest, freshest produce. Our soup selection changes daily, depending on ingredient availability and the creative whimsy of our culinary team. In this section you'll find five of our favorites. Serve them as a first-course for dinner or simply accompany them with a crusty loaf of bread for a light meal.

This cool, refreshing soup is perfect for the hot days of summer.

Chilled Cucumber Coconut Soup

YIELD: 4 TO 6 SERVINGS

CHILI OIL

¼ cups canola oil

½ teaspoon crushed
red chili flakes

¼ teaspoon paprika

CUCUMBER COCONUT SOUP

4 English cucumbers
(each about 1 pound),
sliced into 1-inch rounds

1 can (32 ounces)
coconut milk

1 bunch fresh mint
(about 3 ounces),
chopped

Salt

Freshly ground
black pepper

To make the Chili Oil, combine the oil, chili flakes, and paprika in a small saucepan and bring to a gentle simmer over medium heat. Remove from the heat and let the oil steep for 1 hour. Strain through a fine-mesh strainer into a bowl or storage container.

To make the Cucumber Coconut Soup, combine the cucumbers, coconut milk, and mint in a blender. Process on high speed until completely smooth. Season with salt and pepper to taste. Chill thoroughly before serving.

Garnish each serving of soup with a few drops of the Chili Oil.

Ying Yang Rolls, page 38

Meditteranean Polenta Squares, page 6

Chopped Salad, page 32

Frito Misto, page 12

Pizza Margherita, page 46

Picatta, page 66, with Roasted Garlic Mashed Potatoes, page 80, and Blanched Spinach, page 74

This is a hearty, comforting soup that is full of enticing flavors and aromas. Although it calls for a large quantity of vegetable stock, rest assured that it will cook down considerably and is the correct amount.

White Bean and Escarole Soup

YIELD: 4 TO 6 SERVINGS

2 lemons

½ cup extra-virgin olive oil

¾ cup very finely diced carrot

6 whole garlic cloves, peeled

Salt

Freshly ground black pepper

1 head escarole (about 1½ pounds), chopped into 1-inch pieces

¾ cup finely chopped white onion

2 gallons Blond Vegetable Stock (page 95)

1 cup dried white beans, soaked for 8 to 12 hours and drained

1 bunch flat-leaf parsley (about 3 ounces), chopped

Preheat the oven to 175 degrees F or the lowest setting possible. Remove the yellow outer part of the lemon skin using a citrus zester or fine box grater, being careful not to remove any of the white pith. Arrange the zest on a sheet pan and heat it in the oven until it is very dry. The amount of time this will take will depend on your oven; monitor the zest closely so it does not burn.

While the zest is drying, place the olive oil in a large soup pot over high heat until it just begins to simmer. Add the carrot, garlic, and salt and pepper to taste and cook and stir over high heat for about 5 minutes, until the carrot is soft.

Add the escarole and onion and cook and stir for 5 minutes. Add the stock and beans, lower the heat to medium, cover, and simmer for about 40 minutes, or until the beans are tender.

Taste the soup and add more salt and pepper if needed. Garnish with the dried lemon zest and parsley.

Fresh fennel adds a sophisticated dimension to the pure simplicity of this tomato soup.

Tomato Fennel Soup

YIELD: 4 TO 6 SERVINGS

- 2 tablespoons extra-virgin olive oil

- 2 fennel bulbs (about 1 pound each), sliced

- 1 tablespoon whole coriander seeds

- 1 tablespoon whole fennel seeds

- 1 cup anise-flavored liqueur

- 4 cans (16 ounces each) plum tomatoes, not drained

- Salt

- Freshly ground black pepper

- Fennel fronds

- Extra-virgin olive oil

Heat the oil in a large soup pot. Add the fennel and cook and stir for about 2 minutes, until it is soft. Add the coriander and fennel seeds and cook and stir for 2 minutes, until the seeds are toasted. Carefully add the liqueur to the pot (it will ignite) and cook until the flame goes away.

Add the tomatoes and simmer for 1 hour, stirring occasionally. Season with salt and pepper to taste. Process the soup in batches in a blender on high speed until smooth. Garnish each serving with fennel fronds and a few drops of extra-virgin olive oil.

In Sublime's kitchen, a total of fifty onions are used to make a batch of this rich soup. For this scaled-down version, only five onions are needed.

50 Onion Soup

YIELD: 6 SERVINGS

1 cup canola oil

5 white onions, chopped (about 5 pounds)

1 cup tomato paste

1 tablespoon chopped fresh rosemary

4 cups red wine (not cooking wine)

1 gallon Dark Vegetable Stock (page 94)

6 slices toasted rustic bread

6 slices soy cheese

Place the oil in a heavy-bottomed soup pot and heat. Add the onions and cook and stir for 15 to 20 minutes, until they are deep golden brown. Stir in the tomato paste and rosemary and cook for 5 minutes. Add the red wine and simmer for about 5 minutes, until the liquid is almost gone.

Add the vegetable stock and simmer for 15 minutes. To serve, ladle the hot soup into individual crocks and top each serving with a slice of the toasted bread. Top the toasted bread with a slice of the soy cheese and place the crocks under the broiler until the cheese is melted. Serve immediately.

This velvety soup has just the right amount of intriguing spice.

Carrot Ginger Soup

YIELD: 4 TO 6 SERVINGS

4 tablespoons canola oil

½ cup peeled and sliced fresh ginger

5 pounds carrots, peeled and sliced

1 cup sliced shallots

1 tablespoon whole fenugreek seeds

1 tablespoon whole fennel seeds

3 cups Blond Vegetable Stock (page 95)

3 cups coconut milk

Salt

Freshly ground black pepper

1 tablespoon thinly sliced chives

Heat the oil in a large soup pot. Add the ginger and cook and stir for 2 minutes. Add the carrots and the shallots and cook and stir for 5 to 10 minutes, until the carrots are almost tender. Add the fenugreek and fennel seeds and cook and stir for 2 minutes, until they are toasted.

Add the vegetable stock, cover, and simmer for about 20 minutes, until the carrots are very soft and dark orange. Remove from the heat and stir in the coconut milk. Process the soup in batches in a blender until it is smooth and creamy. Season with salt and pepper to taste. Garnish with the chives.

As soon as you walk in the door, you'll know Sublime is a special place with its waterfalls, greenery, Peter Max paintings, and smart, attentive staff. As you walk to your table you may spot Hollywood celebrities, politicians, or famous musicians and artists.

Salads

Salads seem to revivify the body—and the palate—perhaps more than any other type of dish. Sublime's culinary team has created salad recipes that are uncomplicated in their preparation yet elaborate in their flavor. Whether you're in the mood for a rich, creamy Caesar (a favorite for Sublime guests) or a lively, zingy Chopped Salad, these recipes encompass everything you'd ever crave from a salad!

Contrasting flavors are the focal point
of this stunning salad.

Baby Arugula Salad

YIELD: 4 TO 6 SERVINGS

1 pound bell peppers
(any color)

¾ cup extra-virgin olive oil

¼ cup balsamic vinegar

1 teaspoon Dijon mustard

1 teaspoon chopped shallots

Salt

Freshly ground black pepper

1 pound baby arugula

1 cup chopped walnuts

1 cup pitted
kalamata olives,
sliced in half lengthwise

½ cup golden raisins

Place the bell peppers directly over an open flame or under the broiler and roast until the skin is charred and the peppers are soft. Transfer to a bowl and cover with plastic wrap to steam the peppers and soften their skins.

When the peppers are cool enough to handle, peel off the skins with your fingers and discard. Slice open the peppers and remove the stem and all of the seeds. Slice the peppers into ⅛-inch-wide strips and store in the refrigerator for up to 3 days.

To make the dressing, combine the oil, vinegar, mustard, and shallots in a large bowl. Season with salt and pepper to taste and set aside.

To make the salad, combine the arugula, 1 cup of the roasted bell peppers, and all of the walnuts, olives, and raisins in another large bowl.

Stir the dressing and pour it over the salad, using just enough to coat the ingredients evenly. Toss and serve.

Our signature salad is straightforward
and satisfying.

Caesar

YIELD: 4 TO 6 SERVINGS

1 jar (8 ounces) water-packed
artichoke hearts

2 cups all-purpose flour

Salt

Freshly ground black pepper

1½ cups vegan mayonnaise

4 tablespoons vegan
Worcestershire sauce

4 tablespoons freshly
squeezed lemon juice

2 tablespoons Dijon mustard

2 tablespoons
chopped raw garlic

2 tablespoons Roasted Garlic
(page 91)

2 tablespoons
cracked black pepper

2 heads romaine lettuce
(about 1½ pounds each),
sliced into 1-inch pieces

Drain the artichoke hearts in a mesh sieve and rinse well under running water. Pat them dry with a towel. Spread the flour in a large dish and dip the artichoke hearts into it until they are evenly coated all over. Shake to remove any excess flour.

Deep-fry the artichoke hearts at 350 degrees F for 3 to 5 minutes, until crisp. Remove them from the oil and season with salt and ground pepper to taste. Place the artichoke hearts on paper towels to drain any excess oil.

Combine the mayonnaise, Worcestershire sauce, lemon juice, mustard, raw garlic, Roasted Garlic, and cracked pepper in a large bowl and mix well. Add the romaine lettuce and toss until the leaves are evenly coated. Season with salt to taste and top with the artichoke hearts.

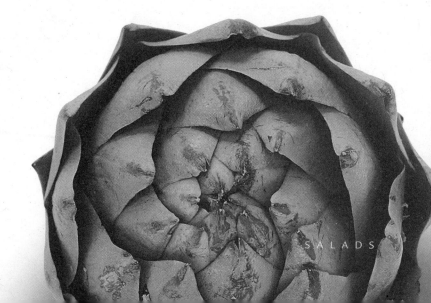

Vivid flavors and colors
make our Chopped Salad a standout.

Chopped Salad

See photo between pages 22 and 23.

YIELD: 4 TO 6 SERVINGS

¾ cup extra-virgin olive oil

¼ cup red wine vinegar

1 tablespoon chopped
fresh oregano

1 tablespoon chopped shallot

1 tablespoon chopped garlic

Salt

Freshly ground black pepper

1 cup cooked or canned
chickpeas, rinsed and drained

1 cup pitted kalamata olives,
sliced in half lengthwise

1 cup diced cucumber

1 cup diced red onion

1 cup diced bell pepper
(any color)

1 cup diced ripe tomato

2 tablespoons sliced scallion

1 head romaine lettuce
(about 1½ pounds),
cut into 1-inch pieces

T o make the dressing, combine the oil, vinegar, oregano, shallot, and garlic in a small bowl and season with salt and pepper to taste. Whisk until well blended.

To make the Chopped Salad, combine the chickpeas, olives, cucumber, onion, bell pepper, tomato, and scallion in a large bowl. Add the dressing and toss until evenly distributed. Arrange the romaine lettuce so it forms "nests" in the bottom of chilled salad bowls and fill with the chopped salad.

Juicy heirloom tomatoes, accented by tangy capers,
are the centerpiece of this salad.

Tomato Carpaccio

YIELD: 4 TO 6 SERVINGS

2 large, ripe heirloom tomatoes
(about 1 pound each),
cut into paper-thin slices

½ cup extra-virgin olive oil

1½ teaspoons salt

1 teaspoon
cracked black pepper

2 cups micro greens or
baby greens

1 cup capers, drained

1 cup fresh basil leaves

Arrange the tomato slices in concentric circles on chilled salad plates until each plate is covered. Drizzle evenly with the olive oil and sprinkle with salt and pepper to taste. Arrange the micro greens and capers around the tomatoes and top with the basil leaves.

Robust watercress, adorned with giant white beans, forms the basis for this distinctive salad.

Watercress Salad

YIELD: 4 TO 6 SERVINGS

½ fennel bulb

1 large onion, peeled and cut into 1-inch-thick slices

1 cup canola oil

Salt

Freshly ground black pepper

¼ cup cabernet vinegar

1 tablespoon grainy mustard

1 tablespoon Roasted Garlic (page 91)

Salt

4 bunches watercress (about 1 pound)

1 cup cooked or canned gigante beans (giant white beans), rinsed and drained

Remove the stalk from the fennel bulb with a sharp knife. Set aside the fronds for garnish. Using a mandolin or electric slicer, cut the fennel into paper-thin slices. Set aside.

Brush the onion slices lightly with ¼ cup of the oil and season with salt and pepper to taste. Grill over high heat (using a grill, cast iron skillet, or griddle) for about 5 minutes per side, until soft. Cut the onion slices into ¼-inch-thick pieces.

To make the dressing, place the vinegar, mustard, and garlic in a blender. Process on high speed while slowly drizzling in the remaining ¾ cup of oil through the cap opening in the lid. The dressing will become thick and creamy. Season with salt and pepper to taste.

Cut off and discard the watercress stems and combine the watercress leaves, beans, grilled onions, and shaved fennel in a large bowl. When ready to serve, add enough dressing to coat the vegetables and toss until evenly distributed.

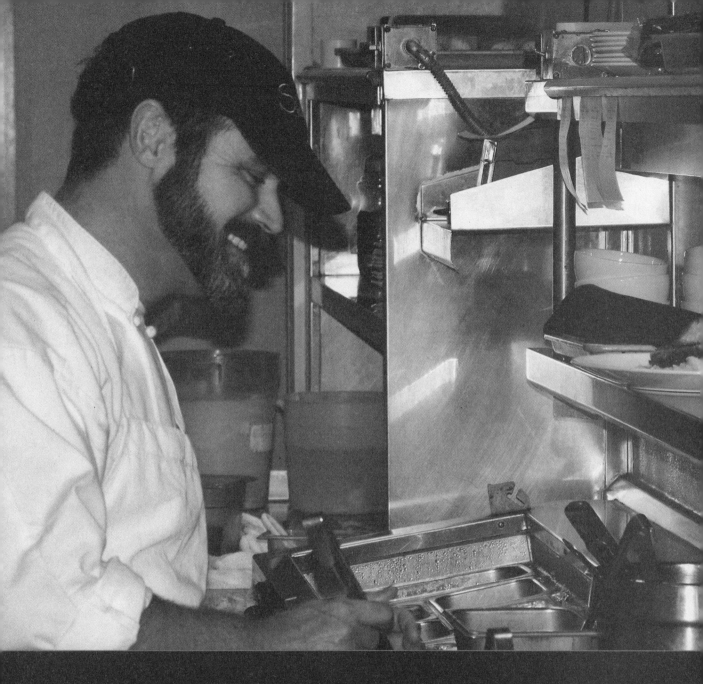

Sublime knows that eating well means feeling good. Each recipe is prepared from the freshest and very best plant-derived ingredients. . . . Your senses will adore the wonderful flavors, and every cell in your body will delight in how good it feels.

Sushi

Sublime's daring sushi menu has more to offer than just adding to the restaurant's hip quotient. These recipes are versatile enough to serve as appetizers or as entrées (except for the Mini Maki, which happens to be a cocktail party crowd pleaser). Whether eaten with chopsticks, fork and knife, or your fingers, these rolls are guaranteed to knock your socks off.

Black rice and tempura form intricate layers
within this visually stunning roll.

Yin Yang Roll

See photo between pages 22 and 23.

YIELD: 4 TO 6 SERVINGS

4 ¼ cups water

Salt

¼ cup ice

4 small asparagus pieces

2 cups black rice

4 sheets nori,
cut in half lengthwise

1 cup soy cream cheese

¼ cup thinly sliced
carrot strips (2 inches long)

4 cups
Tempura Batter (page 89)

1 cup cooked
Sushi Rice (page 87)

1 cup Ponzu Sauce
(page 86)

Place 1 cup of the water and a pinch of salt in a small saucepan and bring to a boil. Mix the ice and 1 cup of the remaining water in a small bowl and set aside. When the water comes to a boil, add the asparagus and cook for 1 minute. Immediately remove the asparagus and submerge it in the ice water. Allow it to cool completely.

Place the black rice and remaining 2 ¼ cups of water in a large saucepan and bring to a boil. Cover, reduce the heat to low, and cook for 10 minutes. Remove from the heat and let stand, covered, for 10 minutes. (The rice will be al dente, similar to wild rice.)

Position 4 of the nori half-sheets with the lines running horizontally. Starting from the bottom, cover about three-quarters of each half-sheet with the black rice, making sure the rice is even and flat. Add a thin line of soy cream cheese (you may use a pastry bag) across the rice.

Layer 1 piece of the asparagus and 1 tablespoon of the carrot over the center of the rice and tightly roll the sheet around the filling, sealing the end with a bit of water. Repeat this process to make a total of 4 rolls.

Dip the rolls in the Tempura Batter and deep-fry in vegetable oil at 350 degrees F for 2 to 3 minutes, until crisp and golden brown. Cover about three-quarters of each of the 4 remaining half-sheets of nori with the sushi rice, making sure the rice is even and flat.

Place a fried roll at the bottom of each sheet in a parallel position. Tightly wrap into a roll, sealing the end with a bit of water. Slice each completed roll into 6 pieces. Serve with the Ponzu Sauce for dipping.

Chives, capers, and creamy vegan mayonnaise
produce a harmony of flavors in this tantalizing roll.

Dynamite Roll

YIELD: 4 TO 6 SERVINGS

4 sheets nori

6 cups Sushi Rice (page 87)

1 cup soy cream cheese

8 avocado strips
(⅛ x ⅛ x 1 inch)

8 cucumber strips
(⅛ x ⅛ x 2 inches)

2 cups vegan mayonnaise

1 cup capers, drained

¼ cup finely diced red onion

2 tablespoons
thinly sliced scallion

2 tablespoons
thinly sliced chives

1 tablespoon
white sesame seeds

1 tablespoon
black sesame seeds

Position the nori sheets with the lines running vertically. Spread a baseball-sized rice ball evenly across each sheet, leaving a ¼-inch margin at the top. Place a line of soy cream cheese (you may use a pastry bag) in the center of the rice and layer on top of it 2 strips of avocado and 2 strips of cucumber. Use a sushi mat to wrap the roll tightly. Place a bit of water on the top margin of the nori to seal it and finish wrapping. Repeat the process with the remaining sheets.

Preheat the oven to 350 degrees F. Combine the mayonnaise, capers, onion, scallion, chives, and white and black sesame seeds in a bowl and mix well. Spread the mixture on a double sheet of foil and bake for about 5 minutes, until it just begins to brown and is piping hot.

Cut each sushi roll into 8 pieces and cover each piece with a dollop of the baked topping. Serve immediately.

Tropical elements converge within the exotic confines of this tempting roll.

Florasian Roll

YIELD: 4 TO 6 SERVINGS

SWEET SOY SAUCE

1 cup brown sugar, firmly packed

1 cup light soy sauce

¼ cup cornstarch

¼ cup water

SUSHI ROLLS

4 sheets nori

6 cups Sushi Rice (page 87)

8 avocado strips (⅛ x ⅛ x 1 inch)

4 cups Tempura Batter (page 89)

8 mango strips (⅛ x ⅛ x 1 inch)

2 ½ cups Aïoli (page 88)

1 cup unsweetened shredded dried coconut

To make the Sweet Soy Sauce, place the sugar and soy sauce in a heavy-bottomed saucepan and bring to a boil while stirring constantly. Combine the cornstarch and water in a small bowl.

When the sugar mixture boils, slowly pour in the cornstarch mixture, stirring constantly with a whisk. Continue to cook and stir until the mixture thickens. Remove from the heat and let cool.

To make the Sushi Rolls, position the nori sheets with the lines running vertically. Evenly spread a baseball-sized rice ball across each sheet, leaving a ¼-inch margin at the top. Place a sushi mat over 1 sheet and carefully flip the mat and nori sheet together so the rice is face down on the mat and the nori is facing up.

Dip the avocado strips in the tempura batter and deep-fry them in vegetable oil at 350 degrees F for 2 to 3 minutes, until crisp.

Place 2 pieces of the avocado, 2 strips of the mango, and a thin line of Aïoli (using a squeeze bottle) on the center of the nori side of the sheet. Wrap the roll tightly with the sushi mat (the rice will be on the outside of the nori). Place a bit of water on the top margin of the nori to seal it and finish wrapping. Repeat the process with each nori sheet.

Sprinkle the coconut evenly on a flat surface. Roll each nori roll in the coconut until it is evenly coated. Cut each roll into 8 pieces. Drizzle the pieces with the Sweet Soy Sauce and serve immediately.

This eye-catching green roll is characterized
by Zen-like balance and simplicity.

Sublime Roll

YIELD: 4 TO 6 SERVINGS

4 sheets nori

6 cups Sushi Rice (page 87)

2 ½ cups Aïoli (page 88)

½ cup thinly sliced scallions

4 teaspoons
black sesame seeds

8 cucumber strips
(⅛ x ⅛ x 2 inches)

½ cup micro greens
or baby greens

8 avocado strips
(⅛ x ⅛ x 1 inch)

4 sheets green soybean paper
(optional)

P osition the nori sheets with the lines running vertically. Evenly
spread a baseball-sized rice ball across each sheet, leaving a ¼-
inch margin at the top. Using a squeeze bottle, place a line of Aïoli
in the center of the rice. Sprinkle 2 tablespoons of the scallions and
1 teaspoon of the sesame seeds over the rice on each sheet.

Place 2 strips of the cucumber, 2 tablespoons of the micro
greens, and 2 strips of the avocado over the center of the rice on
each sheet. Use a sushi mat to wrap each roll tightly. Place a bit of
water on the top margin of the nori to seal it and finish wrapping.
Wrap each roll with 1 sheet of green soybean paper, if using. Slice
each roll into 8 pieces.

This uncomplicated, bite-sized, cucumber-
and-avocado roll functions well as either
a finger food or a light appetizer.

Mini Maki

4 sheets nori,
cut in half lengthwise

6 cups Sushi Rice (page 87)

8 cucumber strips
(⅛ x ⅛ x 2 inches)

8 avocado strips
(⅛ x ⅛ x 1 inch)

1 cup Ponzu Sauce (page 86)

Position the nori sheets with the lines running vertically. Spread a golf-ball-sized rice ball evenly across each sheet, leaving a ¼-inch margin at the top. Place equal amounts of the cucumber and avocado in the center of the rice on each sheet.

Use a sushi mat to wrap each roll tightly. Place a bit of water on the top margin of the nori to seal it and finish wrapping. Cut each roll into 8 pieces. Serve with the Ponzu Sauce for dipping.

Pizzas

Nothing hits the spot quite like a good slice of pizza. Sublime guests can watch our pizza chef at work, preparing each fresh pie by hand before sliding it into our famous brick oven (a focal point of the restaurant). Guests are rapt with attention as their glorious pizza emerges, heated to perfection. Bring the magic to your own home with these recipes (and a pizza stone).

A timeless favorite, this recipe showcases the goodness of our renowned tomato sauce and thin pizza crust.

Pizza Margherita

See photo between pages 22 and 23.

YIELD: 4 TO 6 SERVINGS

2 balls Pizza Dough (page 93)

1 cup Basic Tomato Sauce (page 92)

1¼ cup shredded soy mozzarella cheese

2 tablespoons extra-virgin olive oil

3 tablespoons thinly sliced fresh basil

Place 2 large, round pizza stones in the oven (either side by side or on the top and bottom racks, depending on the oven width) and preheat to 500 degrees F. Roll out each ball of dough into a 15-inch circle.

Ladle the tomato sauce onto the middle of the dough. With the back of the ladle, spread the sauce in concentric circles almost to the edge of the dough, leaving a ¼-inch margin.

Top the dough evenly with the soy cheese. Using a pizza peel, place each pizza onto the pizza stones in the oven. Bake for about 10 minutes, until the cheese melts and the crust is golden brown. Remove from the oven, drizzle the olive oil around the margin of the crust, and sprinkle the basil evenly over the top.

This extraordinary pizza features the earthy flavors of mushrooms and roasted garlic coupled with fresh arugula.

Forest Mushroom Pizza

YIELD: 4 TO 6 SERVINGS

½ cup extra-virgin olive oil

1 cup sliced
button mushrooms

1 cup sliced
oyster mushrooms

1 cup sliced
fresh shiitake mushrooms

¼ cup chopped shallots

¼ cup chopped fresh garlic

1 tablespoon minced
fresh rosemary

1 tablespoon minced
fresh thyme

¼ cup vegan margarine

Salt

Freshly ground black pepper

2 balls Pizza Dough (page 93)

4 tablespoons Roasted Garlic
(page 91)

½ cup baby arugula

1 teaspoon
white truffle oil (optional)

Place the olive oil in a sauté pan. Add all of the mushrooms and cook and stir over high heat for 8 to 10 minutes, until crisp and golden brown. Add the shallots, fresh garlic, rosemary, and thyme and cook and stir for 2 to 3 minutes. Add the margarine and heat until melted. Season with salt and pepper to taste. Transfer to a food processor and pulse for 10 seconds at a time until the mushrooms are finely chopped. Spread on a tray to cool and set aside.

Place 2 large, round pizza stones in the oven (either side by side or on the top and bottom racks, depending on the oven width) and preheat to 500 degrees F. Roll out each ball of dough into a 15-inch circle.

Spread the Roasted Garlic in a thin layer to cover the dough, leaving a ¼-inch margin. Spread the mushroom mixture over the Roasted Garlic, still leaving the ¼-inch margin.

Using a pizza peel, place the pizzas on the stones in the oven. Bake for 7 to 8 minutes, until the crust is golden brown. Remove from the oven and top with the arugula. Drizzle with the truffle oil, if using, and serve.

Our magnificent pesto creates an alluring alternative to tomato-sauce pizzas.

Pesto Pizza

YIELD: 4 TO 6 SERVINGS

PESTO SAUCE

1 cup fresh basil leaves

1 cup extra-virgin olive oil

¼ cup pine nuts

2 tablespoons chopped garlic

Salt

Freshly ground black pepper

PIZZA

2 balls Pizza Dough (page 93)

2 cups Pesto Sauce

1 cup shredded soy mozzarella cheese

2 ripe tomatoes, thinly sliced

2 tablespoons extra-virgin olive oil

To make the Pesto Sauce, combine the basil leaves, oil, pine nuts, and garlic in a food processor and process for about 2 minutes, until smooth. Season with salt and pepper to taste.

To make the pizza, place 2 large, round pizza stones in the oven (either side by side or on the top and bottom racks, depending on the oven width) and preheat to 500 degrees F. Roll out each ball of dough into a 15-inch circle.

Spread the Pesto Sauce in a thin layer to cover the dough, leaving a ¼-inch margin. Sprinkle the soy cheese evenly over the Pesto Sauce. Arrange the tomato slices in a circular pattern over the soy cheese.

Using a pizza peel, place the pizzas on the stones. Bake for 7 to 8 minutes, until the crust is golden brown. Remove from the oven and drizzle with the oil.

Spinach paired with vegan ricotta cheese
imbues this white pizza with a mellow flavor.

Florentine Pizza

YIELD: 4 TO 6 SERVINGS

2 balls Pizza Dough (page 93)

½ cup Roasted Garlic (page 91)

2 ½ cups Tofu Ricotta
(page 85)

1 cup Blanched Spinach
(page 74)

2 tablespoons
extra-virgin olive oil

Salt

Freshly ground black pepper

Place 2 large, round pizza stones in the oven (either side by side or on the top and bottom racks, depending on the oven width) and preheat to 500 degrees F. Roll out each ball of dough into a 15-inch circle.

Spread the Roasted Garlic in a thin layer to cover the dough, leaving a ¼-inch margin. Spread the Tofu Ricotta over the Roasted Garlic and top with the spinach, still leaving the ¼-inch margin.

Using a pizza peel, move the pizzas to the stones in the oven. Bake for 7 to 8 minutes, until the crust is golden brown. Remove from the oven, drizzle with the oil, and season with salt and pepper to taste.

This festive Mexican pizza is perfect for parties.

Seven-Layer Pizza

YIELD: 4 TO 6 SERVINGS

SALSA

1 pound ripe tomatoes, diced

6 tablespoons
finely diced red onion

6 tablespoons
extra-virgin olive oil

6 tablespoons
freshly squeezed lime juice

2 tablespoons
finely diced jalapeño chile

2 tablespoons
chopped fresh cilantro

Salt

Freshly ground black pepper

CHILI SAUCE

½ cup Roasted Garlic (page 91)

½ cup brown sugar

¼ cup sambal oelek
(bottled Thai chili-garlic sauce)

¼ cup freshly
squeezed lemon juice

Salt

To make the Salsa, toss all of the ingredients together in a large bowl.

To make the Chili Sauce, combine all of the ingredients in a blender and process on high speed until smooth.

To make the Guacamole, combine all of the ingredients in a large bowl and mash them together using a potato masher.

To make the Refried Beans, rinse and drain the beans and place them in a large pot. Add the water and bring to a boil over high heat. Lower the heat, cover, and simmer for about 25 minutes, or until tender. Thoroughly drain the beans and deep-fry them for 3 minutes in vegetable oil.

Remove the beans from the vegetable oil, season with salt and pepper to taste, and process them through a food mill or mash them with a potato masher. Heat the olive oil in a sauté pan, add the beans, and cook and stir for 5 to 7 minutes over medium heat, until the beans are creamy.

Place 2 large, round pizza stones in the oven (either side by side or on the top and bottom racks, depending on the oven width) and preheat to 500 degrees F. Roll out each ball of dough into a 15-inch circle.

GUACAMOLE

2 ripe avocados
(about 10 ounces each),
halved, pitted, and peeled

3 tablespoons
finely diced red onion

3 tablespoons
chopped ripe tomato

3 tablespoons
chopped fresh cilantro

3 tablespoons
freshly squeezed lime juice

1 tablespoon
thinly sliced scallion

Salt

Freshly ground black pepper

REFRIED BEANS

2 cups dried red beans,
soaked in water to cover
for 8 to 12 hours

6 cups water

Salt

Freshly ground black pepper

6 tablespoons
extra-virgin olive oil

PIZZA

2 balls Pizza Dough (page 93)

1 cup soy sour cream

¾ cup thinly
sliced romaine lettuce

Spread the Chili Sauce in a thin layer to cover the dough, leaving a ¼-inch margin. Spread a layer of the Refried Beans over the Chili Sauce, still leaving the ¼-inch margin.

Using a pizza peel, move the pizzas to the stones in the oven. Bake for 7 to 8 minutes, until the crust is golden brown. Remove from the oven and top with layers of the Guacamole, Salsa, soy sour cream, and romaine lettuce.

Pastas

Nothing brings people together like a hearty dinner featuring delicious pasta. From Italy to Thailand and right back home, Sublime's pasta selections represent the most-loved noodle dishes from around the world. Whether the featured pasta is durum or rice noodles, elbows or linguini, these recipes will take you on a culinary journey while satisfying all your pasta cravings!

This creamy classic is the epitome
of comfort food.

Mac and "Cheese"

YIELD: 4 TO 6 SERVINGS

4 cups elbow macaroni

1 cup vegan margarine

1 cup all-purpose flour

2 quarts plain
unsweetened soymilk

2½ cups grated
soy cheddar cheese

1 tablespoon Dijon mustard

Salt

Cook the macaroni in boiling water until al dente. Drain and set aside. Melt the margarine in a heavy-bottomed saucepan over medium heat. Stir in the flour and cook and stir over medium heat until it becomes a smooth, thin paste.

Slowly stir in the soymilk. Then stir in the soy cheese. Add the mustard and mix with a wooden spoon until the cheese is completely melted and well incorporated. Remove from the heat and combine the sauce with the macaroni. Season with salt to taste.

Soy crumbles and peas transform this pasta
dish into a scintillating main course. Serve it
with warm rustic bread, if desired.

Fusilli Bolognese

YIELD: 4 TO 6 SERVINGS

4 cups fusilli pasta

6 tablespoons
extra-virgin olive oil

2 tablespoons chopped garlic

¼ cup thinly sliced fresh basil

1 quart Basic Tomato Sauce
(page 92)

2 cups soy crumbles

1 pound ice

1 gallon water

1 cup fresh or frozen
green peas

2 tablespoons thinly sliced
fresh basil

Cook the pasta in boiling water until al dente. Drain and set aside.

To make the sauce, heat the oil in a heavy-bottomed saucepan on high heat. Add the garlic and cook and stir for 30 to 60 seconds, until it just starts to brown. Add the basil and cook and stir for 1 minute. Add the tomato sauce and soy crumbles and simmer for 30 minutes.

While the sauce is simmering, mix the ice and water in a large bowl and set aside. Cook the peas in boiling water with a pinch of salt for 1 to 3 minutes. Drain the peas and immediately submerge them in the ice water. Allow the peas to cool completely.

When ready to serve, drain the peas and add them to the sauce. Toss the pasta with the hot sauce and sprinkle with the fresh basil.

The flavors of Provence flourish in this fancy pasta entrée.

Orecchiette

YIELD: 4 TO 6 SERVINGS

3 ⅔ cups extra-virgin olive oil

2 pints cherry tomatoes

6 tablespoons chopped basil stems and leaves

6 whole garlic cloves, peeled

1 pound fennel bulbs, thinly sliced

1 teaspoon whole fennel seeds

½ cup anise liqueur

1 pound zucchini, sliced into 1-inch-thick rounds

3 tablespoons canola oil

Salt

Freshly ground black pepper

4 cups orecchiette pasta

Preheat the oven to 350 degrees F. Place 3 cups of the olive oil and all of the tomatoes, basil, and whole garlic cloves in a heavy-bottomed saucepan. Cook for 20 minutes, until the tomatoes are soft. Strain the tomatoes, basil, and garlic from the oil. (Save the flavored oil for another use.) Set aside the tomatoes and discard the basil and garlic.

Place 2 tablespoons of the remaining olive oil in a sauté pan and place over high heat. Add the sliced fennel and cook and stir for 3 to 4 minutes, until soft. Add the fennel seeds and cook and stir for 30 seconds, until they are toasted. Carefully add the liqueur (it will ignite) and cook until the flame goes away, about 2 minutes. Reduce the heat to low, cover, and cook for 10 minutes longer, until the fennel is tender. Set aside.

Brush the zucchini lightly with the canola oil and season with salt and pepper to taste. Grill over high heat (using a grill, cast iron skillet, or griddle) for about 5 minutes per side, until soft. Set aside.

Cook the pasta in boiling water until al dente. Drain and set aside.

SAUCE

¼ cup chopped garlic

2 cups shelled fresh fava beans

1 cup chardonnay

1 cup Blond Vegetable Stock
(page 95)

½ cup vegan margarine

To make the sauce, heat the remaining olive oil in a heavy-bottomed saucepan on high heat. Add the chopped garlic and cook and stir for 30 to 60 seconds, until it just starts to brown. Add the beans, reserved tomatoes, fennel, and zucchini and stir until well combined.

Add the wine and cook for about 5 minutes, until the liquid is almost gone. Then add the stock and cook for about 5 minutes, until the liquid is almost gone. Add the margarine and mix it in thoroughly. Remove the sauce from the heat and toss it with the pasta.

This rice noodle dish, with baked tofu and peppers, is an adventurous alternative to typical pasta presentations.

Pad Thai

See photo between pages 86 and 87.

YIELD: 4 TO 6 SERVINGS

THAI SAUCE

2 tablespoons
palm sugar or brown sugar

2 tablespoons tamarind pulp
or freshly squeezed lemon juice

1 cup water

2 ¼ teaspoons chopped
Thai basil

¾ teaspoon peeled and
chopped fresh ginger

BAKED TOFU

1 pound extra-firm tofu

1 cup light soy sauce

¼ cup toasted sesame oil

2 tablespoons chopped garlic

2 tablespoons peeled and
chopped fresh ginger

F or the Thai Sauce, place the sugar and tamarind pulp into a heatproof container. Bring the water to a boil in a small saucepan and pour it over the sugar and tamarind. Stir in the basil and ginger and let steep for 1 hour. Stir vigorously and strain through a sieve into another container.

For the Baked Tofu, preheat the oven to 350 degrees F. Cut the tofu into 1-inch cubes and place them in a deep baking dish. Mix the soy sauce, sesame oil, garlic, and ginger and pour over the tofu. Bake for 15 minutes, until the tofu is golden brown and most of the liquid has been absorbed.

NOODLES

2 cups flat rice noodles

6 tablespoons
toasted sesame oil

2 tablespoons chopped garlic

2 tablespoons peeled and
chopped fresh ginger

2 tablespoons
thinly sliced Thai basil

2 tablespoons
thinly sliced Thai chile

¾ cup thinly sliced carrot strips

½ cup thinly sliced
bell pepper strips (use a mix
of red, yellow, and green)

½ cup mung bean sprouts

1 to 2 tablespoons chopped
unsalted peanuts

For the Noodles, cook the rice noodles in boiling water for 2 minutes, until just barely softened. Drain and set aside. Place the oil in a sauté pan over high heat. Add the garlic and ginger and cook and stir for 30 seconds. Add the basil and chile and cook and stir for 1 minute. Add the carrot strips, bell pepper strips, and tofu and cook and stir for about 3 minutes, until the carrot strips just begin to soften. Add the rice noodles and the Thai Sauce and cook for 2 to 3 minutes, until the noodles are soft. Garnish each serving with the mung bean sprouts and peanuts.

Spicy chili flakes and pungent olives
accentuate this unforgettable linguini dish.

Linguini Puttanesca

See photo between pages 86 and 87.

YIELD: 4 TO 6 SERVINGS

2 red bell peppers

¼ cup extra-virgin olive oil

2 tablespoons chopped garlic

⅔ cup thinly sliced
fresh basil leaves

1 tablespoon
red chili flakes
(use less for a milder flavor)

4 cups Basic Tomato Sauce
(page 92)

1 cup pitted kalamata olives,
sliced in half lengthwise

½ cup capers, drained

4 cups linguini

Place the bell peppers directly over an open flame or under the broiler and roast until the skin is charred and the peppers are soft. Transfer to a bowl and cover with plastic wrap to steam the peppers and soften their skins. When the peppers are cool enough to handle, peel off the skins with your fingers and discard. Slice open the peppers and remove the stem and all of the seeds. Slice the peppers into ⅛-inch-wide strips. (The peppers may be prepared in advance and stored in the refrigerator for up to 3 days.)

Heat the oil in a heavy-bottomed saucepan over high heat. Add the garlic and cook and stir for 30 to 60 seconds, until it just starts to brown.

Add 2 tablespoons of the basil and all of the chili flakes and cook and stir for 30 to 60 seconds. Add the bell peppers, tomato sauce, olives, and capers. Reduce the heat to low and simmer for 30 minutes, stirring occasionally.

While the sauce is simmering, cook the pasta in boiling water until al dente. Drain. Toss the pasta with the hot sauce and garnish with the remaining basil.

While your eyes and taste buds rejoice in the exquisite colors and flavors, your waistline will be trimmer, and your heart will be lighter, too. Sublime is going strong, with devotees flocking to the restaurant on a daily basis. And since the day it opened, all of Sublime's profits have been donated to animal welfare.

Entrées

At last we've come to the pièce de résistance! It's been said that Sublime's entrées epitomize vegan haute cuisine. Our main course offerings work well either preceded by other courses or served with a side dish for a stand-alone gourmet meal. While aspects of Sublime's menu have evolved over the years, these entrées are the mainstays, renowned for their voluminous portions and seductive flavors.

This stir-fry dish features a cavalcade of Asian vegetables over brown rice.

Dancing Buddha

YIELD: 4 SERVINGS

STIR-FRY SAUCE

2 cups soy sauce

1 cup rice wine vinegar

½ cup hot sauce

VEGETABLES, RICE, AND TOFU

7 cups water

1 cup ice

¾ cup broccoli florets

2 cups brown rice

1 teaspoon salt

6 tablespoons toasted sesame oil

2 tablespoons peeled and chopped fresh ginger

2 tablespoons chopped garlic

¾ cup thinly sliced carrot strips

¾ cup sliced water chestnuts

½ cup thinly sliced bell pepper strips (use a mix of red, yellow, and green)

2½ cups sliced tofu or seitan

GARNISH

2 tablespoons thinly sliced scallions

1 tablespoon sesame seeds

To make the Stir-Fry Sauce, combine all of the ingredients in a bowl and set aside.

Mix 3 cups of the water and all of the ice in a large bowl. Cook the broccoli in boiling water with a pinch of salt for 2 minutes. Drain the broccoli and submerge it in the ice water. Allow it to cool completely.

Place the remaining 4 cups of water in a saucepan along with the rice and salt and bring to a boil. Reduce the heat to medium-low, cover, and cook for 40 minutes, until the rice is tender.

Heat the oil in a large sauté pan over high heat. Add the ginger and garlic and cook and stir for 30 seconds. Add the broccoli, carrot strips, water chestnuts, and bell pepper strips, and cook and stir for 4 to 5 minutes, until heated through.

Add the Stir-Fry Sauce and tofu and cook and stir for 5 minutes longer. Serve over the hot rice and garnish with the scallions and sesame seeds.

Reminiscent of an enjoyable country meal, our individual loaves gets a finishing touch from scrumptious onion gravy. If desired, serve each loaf atop a scoop of Creamed Spinach (page 79) and surround the loaf with Roasted Potatoes (page 75).

Sublime Loaf

YIELD: 6 SERVINGS

ONION GRAVY

4 teaspoons canola oil

¾ cup sliced white onion

⅓ cup tomato paste

1⅓ cups Dark Vegetable Stock (page 94)

2¾ tablespoons vegan margarine

Salt

Freshly ground black pepper

LOAVES

2 cups soy crumbles

½ cup tomato juice

½ cup extra-virgin olive oil

1 cup cooked or canned black beans, rinsed and drained

6 tablespoons chopped garlic

¼ cup thinly sliced carrot strips

½ cup sliced water chestnuts

2 tablespoons thinly sliced scallion

½ cup Caramelized Onions (page 90)

To make the Onion Gravy, place the oil in a large pot over high heat. Add the onion and cook and stir for 8 to 10 minutes, until it is caramelized. Add the tomato paste and cook and stir for 2 minutes. Add the stock and simmer for 10 minutes. Transfer to a blender and process on high speed for about 2 minutes, until smooth. Blend in the cold margarine, 1 tablespoon at a time. Pour the blended mixture into a bowl and season with salt and pepper to taste.

To make the Loaves, combine the soy crumbles, tomato juice, and ¼ cup of the oil in a blender and process on high speed for 3 to 5 minutes to make smooth, thick paste. Grind the beans in a food mill or mash them with a potato masher. Combine them with the blended paste and set aside. Place the remaining ¼ cup of olive oil in a pan over high heat. Add the garlic and carrot strips and cook and stir for 2 to 3 minutes, until soft. Add the garlic and carrot strips to the bean mixture and stir in the caramelized onion, water chestnuts, and scallion. Mix well. Using your hands, form into 6 football-shaped loaves, each about 5 x 3 inches.

Preheat the oven to 375 degrees F. Line an 18 x 13-inch sheet pan with parchment paper and place the loaves on top. Cover the pan with foil and bake for 45 minutes. Remove the foil and bake for 15 minutes longer. Remove from the oven and let the loaves cool to room temperature. To serve, gently reheat the Onion Gravy and ladle 4 tablespoons of the gravy over each loaf.

Our signature entrée features breaded seitan cutlets in a delicate lemon-caper sauce. If desired, serve the cutlets atop a scoop of Roasted Garlic Mashed Potatoes (page 80) and layer with Blanched Spinach (page 74).

Picatta

See photo between pages 22 and 23.

YIELD: 4 SERVINGS

LEMON-CAPER SAUCE

2 cups white wine

½ cup chopped shallots

1 cup vegan margarine

½ cup capers, drained

3 tablespoons freshly squeezed lemon juice

Salt

To make the Lemon-Caper Sauce, combine the wine and shallots in a large saucepan and cook and stir over high heat for about 15 minutes, until almost dry. Transfer to a blender and process on high speed for about 2 minutes, until smooth. Gradually blend the cold margarine into the mixture, 2 tablespoons at a time. Pour the sauce into a bowl, stir in the capers and lemon juice, and season with salt to taste.

BREADED SEITAN

1 cup vital wheat gluten

3 tablespoons
nutritional yeast flakes

1 teaspoon garlic powder

1 teaspoon onion powder

1 teaspoon salt,
plus more as needed

1 teaspoon
ground white pepper

6 cups vegetable broth

2 tablespoons Bragg Liquid
Aminos (optional)

1 tablespoon soy sauce

Freshly ground black pepper

2 cups all-purpose flour

To make the Breaded Seitan, combine the vital wheat gluten, nutritional yeast, garlic powder, onion powder, salt, and white pepper in a medium bowl. Combine ¾ cup of the broth, the optional Bragg Liquid Aminos, and the soy sauce in a small bowl. Gently stir this liquid into the vital wheat gluten mixture using your hands and mix until the gluten is rubbery (do not use an electric mixer). Knead the mixture 10 to 15 times, let it rest for 5 minutes, and then knead it again a few more times.

Divide the ball of gluten into 4 chunks. Gently stretch each chunk into a flat cutlet, about ¾ inch thick (the gluten will expand when cooking, so it is important to start with this thin size). Don't worry about any holes that may form in the gluten.

Place the remaining 5¼ cups broth in a large pot, add the gluten cutlets, and bring to a gentle simmer. Cover and cook for at least 1 hour, until the gluten is firm. Remove the cutlets from the pot and pat them dry with a paper towel. Dredge the cutlets in the flour and season with salt and black pepper to taste.

Fry the cutlets in canola oil in a sauté pan for 3 minutes on each side, until they are crisp and golden brown. Be careful not to overcook them or they will become tough. Drizzle each serving with the Lemon-Caper Sauce.

For a gratifying takeoff on meat and potatoes, accompany these delectable portobello circles with a mound of Olive Oil Whipped Potatoes (page 78) and a serving of Blanched Spinach (page 74), topped with three Onion Rings (page 76).

Portobello Tenderloin

See photo between pages 86 and 87.

YIELD: 4 SERVINGS

TOMATO COMFITURE

3 gallons water

Salt

2 pounds ripe tomatoes

½ cup sugar

½ cup apple cider vinegar

4 tablespoons chopped fresh thyme

AU POIVRE SAUCE

1 quart water

6 tablespoons dried porcini mushrooms

2 cups brandy

5 shallots, sliced

1 cup Cashew Cream (page 84)

1 can (3 ounces) green peppercorns, drained

½ cup vegan margarine

Salt

To make the Tomato Comfiture, combine the water and a pinch of salt in a large pot and bring to a boil. Cut an X in the bottom of each tomato and remove the core. Place the tomatoes in the boiling water for 2 to 3 minutes; remove as soon as the skin starts to crack. Immerse the tomatoes in ice water until they are cool.

Peel off the skins using your fingers. Cut the tomatoes in half and squeeze out the seeds. Place the tomatoes, sugar, vinegar, and thyme in a saucepan. Cook for 30 minutes over high heat, stirring almost constantly, until all the water has evaporated and the mixture has the consistency of jam.

To make the Au Poivre Sauce, bring the water to a boil in a medium saucepan and add the porcini mushrooms. Remove from the heat and soak the mushrooms in the hot water for 30 minutes to make a stock.

While the mushrooms are soaking, combine the brandy and shallots in a large saucepan. Cook over high heat for about 2 minutes, until almost all of the liquid has evaporated. Strain the mushroom stock and add it to the shallots. (Reserve the mushrooms for another use, if desired.) Add the Cashew Cream and peppercorns and cook over high heat for 10 to 15 minutes, until slightly thickened. Transfer the sauce to a blender along with the margarine and process on high speed until smooth. Season with salt to taste and process again briefly.

PORTOBELLO TENDERLOINS

1 cup canola oil

Salt

Freshly ground black pepper

8 portobello mushrooms
(about 2 ounces each),
stems and gills removed

6 tablespoons
chopped fresh garlic

To make the Portobello Tenderloins, preheat the oven to 350 degrees F. Pour the oil into a bowl and season it with salt and pepper to taste. Dip the mushrooms into the oil mixture, arrange them on a baking sheet, and bake for 15 minutes. Let cool to room temperature. Keep the oven on.

Take one mushroom and press a 2½-inch ring mold over it, cutting the mushroom into a circle. Leaving the mushroom circle in the ring, remove the excess mushroom from the outside of the ring mold and set it aside. Repeat this process for the remaining mushrooms until you have 8 circles in ring molds with the excess set aside.

Place 4 of the mushroom circles in individual rings molds. Evenly distribute the excess mushroom pieces around the inside walls of the molds on top of the mushroom circles. Place 6 tablespoons of the Tomato Comfiture in the center of each of the ring molds. Place the remaining 4 mushroom circles over the Tomato Comfiture. Bake in the oven (at 350 degrees F) for 10 minutes.

To serve, place each ring mold on a plate and carefully lift it straight up to release the mushrooms. Cover the mushrooms with the Au Poivre Sauce and serve.

This superb "steak" is topped with a watercress salad. If desired, serve it over Couscous (page 77).

Grilled Seitan Steak

YIELD: 4 SERVINGS

TZATZIKI SAUCE

⅓ cup seeded and coarsely chopped cucumber

2 teaspoons chopped garlic

½ cup plain soy yogurt

2 tablespoons freshly squeezed lemon juice

2 teaspoons chopped fresh mint

Salt

Freshly ground black pepper

SEITAN STEAK

1 cup vital wheat gluten

1 teaspoon garlic powder

1 teaspoon onion powder

1 teaspoon salt

1 teaspoon freshly ground black pepper

6 cups vegetable broth

2 tablespoons soy sauce

2 tablespoons Bragg Liquid Aminos (optional)

1 tablespoon vegetarian Worcestershire sauce

To make the Tzatziki Sauce, combine the cucumber and garlic in a food processor and process until smooth. Drain in cheesecloth for 8 to 12 hours. Combine the drained cucumber mixture with the yogurt, lemon juice, and mint and season with salt and pepper to taste.

To make the Seitan Steak, combine the vital wheat gluten, garlic powder, onion powder, salt, and pepper in a medium bowl. Combine ¾ cup of the broth and all of the soy sauce, optional Bragg Liquid Aminos, and Worcestershire sauce in a small bowl. Gently stir this liquid into the vital wheat gluten mixture using your hands and mix until the gluten is rubbery (do not use an electric mixer). Knead the mixture 10 to 15 times, let it rest for 5 minutes, and then knead it again a few more times.

Divide the ball of gluten into 4 chunks. Gently stretch each chunk into a flat cutlet, about ¾ inch thick (the gluten will expand when cooking, so it is important to start with this thin size). Don't worry about any holes that may form in the gluten.

Place the remaining broth in a large pot, add the gluten cutlets, and bring to a gentle simmer. Cover and cook for at least 1 hour, until the gluten is firm. Remove the cutlets from the pot and pat them dry with a paper towel. Season with salt and pepper to taste.

Grill each cutlet for 3 minutes per side over medium heat (use a grill, cast iron skillet, or griddle). Slice each cutlet into 5 thin, angled strips.

WATERCRESS SALAD

½ small red onion

1 cup watercress

1 tablespoon
extra-virgin olive oil

Salt

GARNISH

½ cup chopped
raw almonds (with skins)

To make the Watercress Salad, use a mandolin or a sharp knife to slice the onion into paper-thin slices. Combine the onion, watercress, oil, and salt to taste in a large bowl.

To serve, fan out 5 seitan strips on each plate. Place a few dollops of the Tzatziki Sauce at the side of the seitan. Arrange the Watercress Salad on top of the seitan and sprinkle with the almonds.

Sides

Enhance your favorite main dishes with these adaptable side dishes. Feel free to create a whole meal from multiple sides, as some guests do when dining at Sublime.

Blanched Spinach

See photo between pages 22 and 23, 86 and 87.

YIELD: 2 CUPS

1 pound ice

2 gallons water

Salt

1 pound fresh spinach

Mix the ice and 1 gallon of the water in a large bowl and set aside.

Pour the remaining gallon of water into a large pot. Add a pinch of salt and bring to a boil. Submerge the spinach in the boiling water and cook for 2 minutes.

Drain the spinach and immediately submerge it in the ice water. Let cool completely. Reheat the spinach gently when ready to serve.

Roasted Potatoes

YIELD: ABOUT 2 CUPS

12 red bliss potatoes
(about 1 pound),
cut in half

1 teaspoon finely
chopped fresh rosemary

1 teaspoon finely
chopped fresh thyme

Salt

Freshly ground black pepper

½ cup extra-virgin olive oil

8 whole garlic cloves,
peeled

Preheat the oven to 350 degrees F. Place the potatoes on a baking sheet and season them with the rosemary and thyme. Sprinkle with salt and pepper to taste and drizzle with the oil until evenly coated. Scatter the garlic cloves among the potatoes and bake for 15 to 20 minutes, until the potatoes are tender.

Onion Rings

See photo between pages 86 and 87.

4 large onions
(about 3 pounds), peeled and
sliced into ½-inch-thick rounds

4 cups Tempura Batter
(page 89)

Salt

Separate the onion rounds into rings. Dip the rings in the batter and deep-fry them in vegetable oil at 350 degrees F for 2 to 3 minutes, until golden brown. Remove them from the oil, season with salt to taste, and drain on paper towels.

Couscous

YIELD: ABOUT 6 CUPS

3 cups water

2 cups Israeli couscous

¼ cup vegan margarine

Salt

Freshly ground black pepper

Place the water and couscous in a large pot and bring to a boil over high heat. Reduce the heat to medium-low, cover, and cook for 10 to 15 minutes, until tender. Add the margarine and season with salt and pepper to taste. Stored in a covered container in the refrigerator, leftover Couscous will keep for up to 2 days.

Olive Oil Whipped Potatoes

See photo between pages 86 and 87.

YIELD: ABOUT 10 CUPS

4 pounds whole
russet potatoes, peeled

Salt

2 cups extra-virgin olive oil

Fill a large pot with water. Add the potatoes and a pinch of salt and bring to a boil over high heat. Reduce the heat and simmer for about 25 minutes, until a knife can be easily inserted into the potatoes. Place the warm potatoes in a food mill and grind them into a bowl. Alternatively, place the potatoes in a bowl and mash them well with a potato masher. Mix in the oil with a whisk and season with salt to taste. Stored in a covered container in the refrigerator, Olive Oil Whipped Potatoes will keep for up to 3 days.

Creamed Spinach

YIELD: ABOUT 5 CUPS

¼ cup vegan margarine

¼ cup all-purpose flour

1 cup plain
unsweetened soymilk

2 cups Blanched Spinach
(page 74)

2 cups Caramelized Onions
(page 90)

Salt

Freshly ground black pepper

Melt the margarine in a large saucepan. Stir in the flour to make a paste. Whisk in the soymilk until smooth and cook over high heat for 1 to 2 minutes, stirring constantly, until thickened. Mix in the spinach and onions and season with salt and pepper to taste. Stored in a covered container in the refrigerator, leftover Creamed Spinach will keep for up to 3 days.

Roasted Garlic Mashed Potatoes

See photo between pages 22 and 23.

YIELD: ABOUT 10 CUPS

4 pounds whole
russet potatoes, peeled

Salt

2 cups Roasted Garlic
(page 91)

1 cup vegan margarine

Fill a large pot with water. Add the potatoes and a pinch of salt and bring to a boil over high heat. Reduce the heat and simmer for about 25 minutes, until a knife can be easily inserted into the potatoes. Place the warm potatoes in a food mill and grind them into a bowl. Alternatively, place the potatoes in a bowl and mash them well with a potato masher. Mix in the roasted garlic and margarine with a whisk and season with salt to taste. Stored in a covered container in the refrigerator, Roasted Garlic Mashed Potatoes will keep for up to 3 days.

Nanci wanted to create a restaurant that would show that plant-based food could indeed be sublime. She meticulously planned all of the details to create an unforgettable, one-of-a-kind destination for food lovers. Four years of hard work later, Nanci's vision became a breathtaking reality: Sublime was born.

Fillings, Toppings, and More Sauces

In this section you'll find the vital components
that are used throughout the book. You may
even want to integrate them into any
other recipes as vegan substitutes.

Cashew Cream

See photo between pages 86 and 87.

YIELD: 3 CUPS

2 cups raw cashews

1 cup water

Combine the cashews and water in a blender and process on high speed until smooth. Stored in a covered container in the refrigerator, Cashew Cream will keep for up to 5 days.

Tofu Ricotta

YIELD: ABOUT 3 CUPS

1 pound extra-firm tofu,
cut into 1-inch cubes

½ cup Cashew Cream (left)

6 tablespoons
chopped fresh parsley

4 tablespoons
freshly squeezed lemon juice

Salt

Freshly ground black pepper

G rind the tofu in a food mill. Alternatively, pulse the tofu in a food processor until finely ground. Transfer the tofu to a large bowl and stir in the Cashew Cream, parsley, and lemon juice. Season with salt and pepper to taste. Stored in a covered container in the refrigerator, Tofu Ricotta will keep for up to 4 days.

Ponzu Sauce

YIELD: 1¾ CUPS

1 cup rice wine vinegar

½ cup soy sauce

¼ cup freshly
squeezed key lime juice

Combine all of the ingredients. Stored in a sealed container or glass jar in the refrigerator, Ponzu Sauce will keep for up to 1 month.

Pad Thai, page 58

Portobello Tenderloin, page 68, with Olive Oil Whipped Potatoes, page 78, Blanched Spinach, page 74, and topped with Onion Rings, page 76

Linguini Puttanesca, page 6C

Coconut Cake, page 100

Baked Apple Napoleon, page 99, topped with Cashew Cream, page 84

Pomtini, page 107

Sushi Rice

YIELD: 6 CUPS

2 cups sushi rice

2 ¼ cups water

¼ cup rice wine vinegar

1 tablespoon sugar

1 teaspoon salt

R inse the sushi rice in a colander under cold water until the water runs clear. Place the rice and the water in a pot and bring to a boil. Lower the heat, cover, and cook for 15 minutes.

Combine the vinegar, sugar, and salt in a small bowl or cup.

When the rice is finished cooking, spread it on a baking sheet, carefully pour the vinegar mixture over it, and gently stir (taking care not to mash the rice). Cool the rice to room temperature and use immediately.

Aïoli

YIELD: 2½ CUPS

2 cups vegan mayonnaise

¼ cup freshly
squeezed lemon juice

2 tablespoons
Roasted Garlic (page 91)

Salt

C ombine the mayonnaise, lemon juice, and Roasted Garlic in a bowl. Season with salt to taste. Stored in a covered container in the refrigerator, Aïoli will keep for up to 4 days.

Tempura Batter

YIELD: ABOUT 4 CUPS

1 cup all-purpose flour

1 cup rice flour

1 teaspoon baking powder

1 teaspoon baking soda

2 to 3 cups ice-cold
soda water

Place the all-purpose flour, rice flour, baking powder, and baking soda in a mixing bowl. Add 2 cups of the soda water and mix just until it is well incorporated. (Do not mix it excessively; it is fine if there are lumps in the batter.) If the mixture is too thick, gradually add the remaining soda water until the batter is the consistency of syrup. Stored in a covered container in the refrigerator, Tempura Batter will keep for up to 1 week.

Caramelized Onions

¼ cup canola oil

2 large onions
(about 10 ounces each),
diced

Salt

Heat the oil in a large sauté pan over high heat until it begins to shimmer. Add the onions and cook over high heat for 10 to 15 minutes, stirring every 2 minutes, until they turn dark golden brown. Remove from the heat and season with salt to taste. Stored in a covered container in the refrigerator, Caramelized Onions will keep for up to 2 days.

Roasted Garlic

YIELD: 4 CUPS

2 cups whole
garlic cloves, peeled

2 cups extra-virgin olive oil

Place the garlic cloves in a heavy-bottomed saucepan and cover with the oil. Bring to a boil, reduce the heat to medium, and cook for 20 minutes, until the garlic is golden brown.

Strain the garlic through a sieve. (You may save the garlic-flavored oil to drizzle over other dishes.) Process the garlic in a food processor or blender until it is smooth. Stored in a covered container in the refrigerator, Roasted Garlic will keep for up to 4 days.

Basic Tomato Sauce

YIELD: 1 GALLON

1 ½ cups extra-virgin olive oil

1 cup finely diced onions

½ cup chopped garlic

2 tablespoons dried basil

2 tablespoons dried oregano

2 tablespoons dried parsley

1 can (4 ounces)
tomato paste

1 cup red wine

1 can (64 ounces)
plum tomatoes, undrained

Salt

Freshly ground black pepper

1 cup chopped
fresh basil leaves

P lace ½ cup of the oil and all of the onions in a large pot. Cook and stir over medium heat for 5 to 7 minutes, until the onions are soft. Add the garlic and cook and stir for 2 to 3 minutes. Add the dried basil, oregano, and parsley and cook and stir for 2 minutes, until the herbs are lightly toasted. Stir in the tomato paste and cook and stir for 2 to 3 minutes, until it turns a rusty color.

Stir in the wine and cook for 10 minutes, or until the liquid is almost gone. Add the tomatoes and simmer for 30 to 35 minutes, stirring occasionally. Season with salt and pepper to taste.

Remove from the heat and stir in the fresh basil leaves and the remaining cup of oil. Crush the tomatoes with a potato masher until they are chunky. Stored in a covered container in the refrigerator, Basic Tomato Sauce will keep for up to 4 days.

Pizza Dough

YIELD: 12 CRUSTS

3 cups water

2 tablespoons sugar

1 tablespoon dry active yeast

6 ½ cups all-purpose flour

¾ cup extra-virgin olive oil

3 tablespoons salt

Mix the water, sugar, and yeast with an electric stand mixer for about 1 minute. Let the mixture rise for about 15 minutes. Add the flour, oil, and salt and mix until it forms a dough.

Divide the dough into 12 equal balls and let rest for 15 minutes. Use the dough immediately or refrigerate the balls in separate zipper-lock bags for up to 1 day. Alternatively, store the dough in the freezer for up to 1 month; thaw it before using.

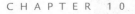

Dark Vegetable Stock

YIELD: ABOUT 8 QUARTS

1 pound chopped
white onions

1 cup chopped carrot

1 cup chopped celery

2 tablespoons canola oil

2 bay leaves

6 tablespoons
chopped parsley

1 tablespoon
whole black peppercorns

8 quarts cold water

Preheat the oven to 400 degrees F. Place the vegetables in a roasting pan, add the oil, and toss until they are evenly coated. Bake, uncovered, for 15 minutes, until they are golden brown.

Transfer the vegetables to a large, heavy-bottomed saucepan and add the bay leaves, parsley, and peppercorns. Cover with the water and bring to a boil. Reduce the heat to low and simmer for 1 hour.

Remove the stock from the heat and strain it. Let cool to room temperature. Stored in a sealed container, Dark Vegetable Stock will keep for up to 4 days in the refrigerator or 4 months in the freezer.

Blond Vegetable Stock

YIELD: ABOUT 2 GALLONS

1 pound chopped
white onions

1 cup chopped carrot

1 cup chopped celery

6 tablespoons
chopped fresh parsley

2 bay leaves

1 tablespoon
whole white peppercorns

8 quarts cold water

Combine the onions, carrot, celery, parsley, bay leaves, and peppercorns in a heavy-bottomed saucepan and add the parsley, bay leaves, and peppercorns. Cover with the water and bring to a boil. Reduce the heat to low and simmer for 1 hour.

Remove the stock from the heat and strain it. Let cool to room temperature. Stored in a sealed container, Blond Vegetable Stock will keep for up to 4 days in the refrigerator or 4 months in the freezer.

Desserts

Vegans and nonvegans alike are astounded by Sublime's desserts. These wondrous confections are a fantastic finale to a singular meal or an inspiring choice for a coffee klatch. We highly recommend that you share the splendor of these desserts with all of your loved and liked ones!

Stewed peaches sweetened with brown sugar make a sweet, seasonal treat.

Georgia Peach Crisp

YIELD: 8 SERVINGS

1 cup brown sugar

1½ cups all-purpose flour

1½ cups vegan margarine

4 pounds fresh peaches, peeled, pitted, and cut into wedges

1 cup sugar (or a little less if the peaches are very sweet)

½ cup all-purpose flour

Soy vanilla ice cream (optional)

U sing your hands, combine the brown sugar, 1 cup of the flour, and ½ cup of the margarine together in a bowl until the mixture forms small crumbs. Set aside.

Melt the remaining cup of margarine in a large saucepan over medium heat. Add the peaches and sugar and cook for 10 to 15 minutes, until the peaches are tender. Add the remaining ½ cup of flour and cook for 5 minutes longer, until the mixture boils and thickens. Remove from the heat and drain off any excess liquid through a sieve.

Preheat the oven to 350 degrees F. Divide the peaches into eight 8-ounce ramekins and top them with the reserved brown sugar mixture. Bake for 5 to 7 minutes, until golden brown. If desired, serve with a scoop of soy vanilla ice cream. Covered and stored in the refrigerator, leftover Georgia Peach Crisp will keep for up to 3 days.

Apples simmered in rum and sweetened with molasses are nestled under flaky phyllo dough in this sensuous dessert.

Baked Apple Napoleon

See photo between pages 86 and 87.

YIELD: 4 TO 6 SERVINGS

½ cup vegan margarine

2 pounds Granny Smith apples, cored, peeled, and sliced

1 cup dark rum

1 cup dark brown sugar, firmly packed

1 cup currants

1 teaspoon ground cinnamon

1 box (approximately 20 sheets) phyllo dough, thawed

1 cup vegan margarine, melted

Melt the ½ cup of margarine in a large saucepan over medium heat. Add the apples, rum, and sugar and cook for 10 to 15 minutes, until the apples are tender. Add the currants, stir, and remove from the heat. Stir in the cinnamon and let the apples cool to room temperature.

Preheat the oven to 350 degrees F. Remove the phyllo dough from the box and unroll it. Remove half of the sheets and lay them into a flat stack on a cutting board. (Refreeze the unused sheets.) Cut the stack into four 2 x 12-inch blocks. Peel off strips of the phyllo dough from the blocks and place 10 overlapping strips in a 4 x 12 x 5-inch baking dish. Brush the strips with some of the melted margarine. Layer one-quarter of the apples over the strips, layer another 10 strips of overlapping phyllo dough over the apples, and brush the strip with some of the melted margarine. Repeat this layering process until all of the apples are in the dish and a final layer of phyllo dough is on top. Bake for 12 to 15 minutes, until the top layer of the phyllo dough is golden brown. Stored in a covered container in the refrigerator, leftover Baked Apple Napoleon will keep for up to 3 days.

Coconut icing and delicate almond cookies embellish this lavish yellow cake.

Coconut Cake

See photo between pages 86 and 87.

YIELD: 8 SERVINGS

ALMOND COOKIES

¼ cup ground almonds

¼ cup unsweetened shredded dried coconut

¼ cup vegan margarine

¼ cup sugar

COCONUT ICING

5 tablespoons vegetable shortening

5 tablespoons vegan margarine

¼ cup plain soymilk

1¾ cup confectioners' sugar

2 cups unsweetened shredded dried coconut

1 teaspoon vanilla extract

To make the Almond Cookies, preheat the oven to 350 degrees F. Combine all of the ingredients to make a firm paste. Form the paste into 8 equal-sized balls using about 4 tablespoons per ball and place them several inches apart on a nonstick baking sheet. Bake for 7 to 8 minutes, until they are golden brown. Transfer to a cooling rack to cool.

To make the Coconut Icing, combine the shortening, margarine, and soymilk in a bowl and beat on high speed using an electric hand blender or small stand mixer. Add the confectioners' sugar and beat for about 3 minutes, until the mixture is smooth. Add the coconut and vanilla extract and beat for 2 minutes longer.

YELLOW CAKE

1¾ cups sugar

10 tablespoons
vegan margarine

2 cups all-purpose flour

1 teaspoon powdered
vegan egg replacer

1 teaspoon salt

½ teaspoon baking soda

¾ cup plain soymilk

1½ teaspoons vanilla extract

¾ cup water

To make the Yellow Cake, preheat the oven to 350 degrees F. Mist two 9-inch round cake pans with nonstick cooking spray. Combine the sugar and margarine in a bowl and beat with a mixer or hand blender on high for about 2 minutes. Sift together the flour, egg replacer, salt, and baking soda and beat half of this mixture into the sugar mixture. Next, beat the soymilk and vanilla extract into the sugar mixture. Then beat in the remainder of the dry ingredients. Finally, beat in the water.

Divide the batter equally between the prepared cake pans and bake for 20 minutes (until a toothpick inserted into the center of each cake comes out clean). Cool the cakes to room temperature before removing them from the pans. Frost with the Coconut Icing and garnish with the Almond Cookies. Stored tightly covered in the refrigerator, leftover Coconut Cake and Almond Cookies will keep for up to 3 days.

A campfire classic gets a classy reinterpretation in this decadent dessert.

S'mores Brownies

YIELD: 4 TO 6 SERVINGS

GRAHAM CRACKER CRUST

1 cup vegan
graham cracker crumbs

½ cup vegan margarine, melted

BROWNIE BATTER

1 cup cake flour

½ cup unsweetened
cocoa powder

1 tablespoon baking powder

1 cup plain soymilk

1 cup dark brown sugar,
firmly packed

1 cup vegan chocolate chips

S'MORES TOPPING
AND GARNISH

1 tub (10 ounces)
Ricemellow Crème

Confectioners' sugar

To make the Graham Cracker Crust, combine the graham cracker crumbs and margarine in a large mixing bowl and mix thoroughly using your hands. Set aside.

To make the Brownie Batter, sift the flour, cocoa powder, and baking powder together in a mixing bowl. Add the soymilk, brown sugar, and chocolate chips and beat with a mixer or hand blender.

Preheat the oven to 350 degrees F. Line a 9½ x 12-inch baking pan with parchment paper and evenly spread the graham cracker mixture over the bottom to form a crust. Pour in the batter and bake for 20 minutes (until a toothpick inserted in the center comes out clean).

Cut into 1 x 3-inch pieces. Spread 2 tablespoons of the Ricemellow Crème on top of each square. Heat the Ricemellow Crème with a blowtorch, until it is dark golden brown. Serve on dishes sprinkled with confectioners' sugar. Stored in a covered container in the refrigerator, leftover S'mores Brownies will keep for up to 3 days.

This heavenly concoction made from brown rice, raisins, and soymilk is simply delightful— and delightfully simple!

Brown Rice Pudding

YIELD: 4 TO 6 SERVINGS

1 cup water

¼ cup brown rice

Salt

3 cups plain soymilk

1 cup golden raisins

1 cup black seedless raisins

1 cup light brown sugar, firmly packed

Place the water, rice, and a pinch of salt in a saucepan and bring to a boil. Reduce the heat to medium-low, cover, and cook for 10 to 15 minutes.

Combine the rice and soymilk in a large pot. Stir in the golden raisins, black raisins, and sugar. Cover and cook over low heat, stirring occasionally, for about 1 hour, or until most of the soymilk has been absorbed and the rice is creamy. Serve warm. Stored in a covered container in the refrigerator, leftover Brown Rice Pudding will keep for up to 3 days.

Cocktails

Sublime's bar is a favorite hobnobbing spot for our cool, eclectic denizens. The bar (constructed out of recycled glass) offers a vantage point of the entire restaurant, while a giant hi-def screen displaying natural imagery serves as the bar's backdrop. But the cocktails themselves are definitely the star attraction. Quench your thirst with these exotic elixirs and you'll see what the fuss is all about!

Startle the senses with this refreshing, Zen-like drink.

Green Tea Martini

YIELD: 2 MARTINIS

¼ cup green tea vodka

Splash of green tea liqueur

1 lemon wedge

Agave syrup (to serve)

Lemon slices

Pour the vodka and liqueur into a martini shaker filled with ice. Squeeze the lemon wedge into the shaker and shake vigorously. Pour into chilled martini glasses laced with agave syrup and garnish with lemon slices.

This super-fruity cocktail packs a flavorful punch.

Pomtini

See photo between pages 86 and 87.   YIELD: 2 MARTINIS

¼ cup pomegranate vodka

2 tablespoons
pomegranate juice

Splash of Simple Syrup
(page 111)

1 lemon wedge

 our the vodka, juice, and syrup into a martini shaker filled with ice. Squeeze the lemon wedge into the shaker and shake vigorously. Pour the mixture into chilled martini glasses.

This tropical martini promises to take
your taste buds to faraway places.

Lychee Martini

YIELD: 2 MARTINIS

¼ cup vodka

¼ cup lychee juice

Canned or fresh lychee

Pour the vodka and juice into a martini shaker filled with ice and shake vigorously. Pour into chilled martini glasses and garnish with lychee.

This crisp cucumber concoction makes one cool cocktail.

English Cucumber Martini

YIELD: 2 MARTINIS

4 slices peeled English cucumber, plus additional slices for garnish

1 tablespoon Simple Syrup (page 111)

3 lime wedges

¼ cup gin

Place the cucumber, syrup, and lime in a martini shaker. Press the ingredients with a muddling stick or small wooden pestle. Pour the gin into the shaker and shake vigorously. Strain into chilled martini glasses and garnish with additional cucumber slices.

This luxurious sangria will draw a crowd at your next get-together.

Sublime Sangria

YIELD: 4 TO 6 SERVINGS

1 bottle (750 milliliters)
red Zinfandel

1 orange, sliced
into wedges and seeded

1 lemon, sliced
into wedges and seeded

1 lime, sliced
into wedges and seeded

6 large strawberries, sliced

1 cup blueberries,
sliced in half

1 medium red apple,
cored and sliced into wedges

1 kiwi, peeled
and sliced into wedges

2 tablespoons sugar

2 tablespoons brandy
(optional)

Ginger ale

Orange wedges

Pour the wine into a 2-quart pitcher. Squeeze the juice from the orange, lemon, and lime wedges into the wine. Add the squeezed citrus wedges, strawberries, blueberries, apple, kiwi, sugar, and optional brandy. Stir and refrigerate for 8 to 12 hours. To serve, pour the mixture over ice and splash it with ginger ale. Garnish each serving with an orange wedge.

Simple Syrup

YIELD: VARIES

Water

Granulated sugar

Using a ratio of 1 part water to 2 parts sugar, heat the water in a saucepan and gradually stir in the sugar. Once the sugar has dissolved completely, remove the mixture from the heat and allow it to cool to room temperature. Pour the cooled mixture into a bottle. Stored in a sealed bottle in the refrigerator, Simple Syrup will keep indefinitely.

Many gourmet cookbooks delight the taste buds, only to make your scale groan. On the contrary, these meals are remarkable for the incredible nutrition they bring to your plate. We hope you enjoy these exquisite recipes. Each one is truly sublime.